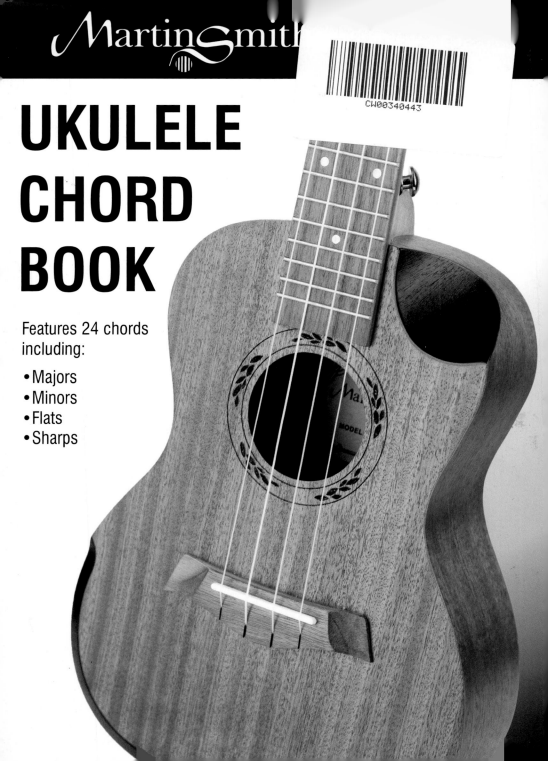

Martin Smith

UKULELE CHORD BOOK

Features 24 chords including:

- Majors
- Minors
- Flats
- Sharps

Uke'n Play
Supa Easy Ukulele

WISE PUBLICATIONS
part of The Music Sales Group
London / New York / Paris / Sydney / Copenhagen / Berlin / Madrid / Hong Kong / Tokyo

Published by
Wise Publications
14-15 Berners Street, London W1T 3LJ, UK.

Exclusive Distributors:
Music Sales Limited
Distribution Centre, Newmarket Road, Bury St Edmunds, Suffolk IP33 3YB, UK.
Music Sales Pty Limited
20 Resolution Drive, Caringbah, NSW 2229, Australia.

Order No. AM1001781
ISBN: 978-1-84938-728-6
This book © Copyright 2010 Wise Publications,
a division of Music Sales Limited.

Created, compiled and edited by Mike Jackson, Diane Jackson (Hill)
and Flying Wombat Music. Melbourne, Australia 2009.
Original design by Ben Lurie.

Printed in the EU.

Play-along CD
Created by Toe Tapper Records.
Mike Jackson – lead vocals, ukulele, melodeon, mountain dulcimer.
Diane Jackson – lead ukulele most tracks.
Thom Jackson – lead ukulele and lead vocals/harmonies on some tracks.
Hugh McDonald – electric bass, guitar, mandolin, fiddle, vocal harmonies.
Ian Blake – keyboards, horns, tin whistle, harmonies and funny vocals.
Recorded at Hugh McDonald's Studio, Melbourne, Australia 2009.
Recorded, Engineered and Mixed by Hugh McDonald.

www.musicsales.com

Contents

Know Your Ukulele

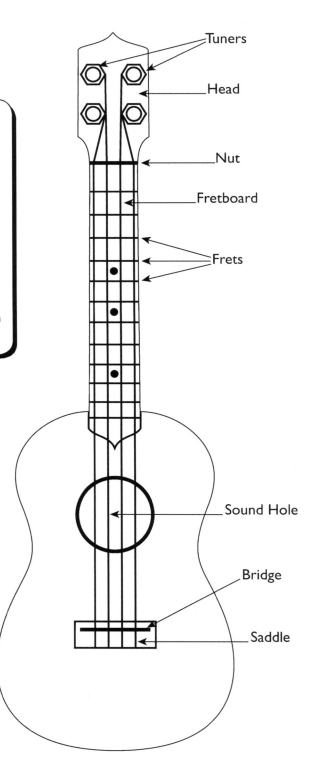

Tuners

Head

Nut

Fretboard

Frets

Sound Hole

Bridge

Saddle

Getting Started Checklist

- Buy a good ukulele
- Ask your music shop to install a strap button
- Make or buy a thin shoulder strap and fit it
- Buy an electronic tuner
- Stretch and tune your ukulele's strings
- Apply coloured dots to your ukulele fretboard as shown on the back cover and page 6

Tuning GCEA

Methods

For good musical ears:

Tuning Track (Track 26)

Play the open* strings, starting from the string closest to your head. Turn the tuning peg a little at first, to check which way you turn to make the string higher or lower. Tune the string to the correct note.

* 'open' means no fingers pressing the strings to the fretboard

Piano

G - first G above middle C

C - middle C

E - first E above middle C

A - first A above middle C

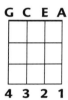

If you find tuning difficult:

Electronic Tuner (available from music stores or www.mikejackson.com.au)

Ask the shop staff to help you with the first tune-up. A clip-on tuner is the best option as it takes only the note from the ukulele and is not affected by other sounds in the immediate area.

To remember the notes for tuning the uke: sing 'My Dog Has Fleas'

Left Handed Players

The ukulele can be easily changed into a left-handed instrument, by swapping the two middle strings over. The outside strings are the same thickness so these don't need to be swapped.

Now tune the ukulele to A E C G as shown .

Strum with the left hand and chord with the right.

The finger positions will be the reverse of those pictured for right-handers and your ukulele will face the opposite direction!

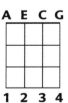

Find the left-handed 'instant play' set up at www.mikejackson.com.au

Other options for left handers: see page 9.

Mike Jackson's Instant Play Method

This system is simple - but it works! It helps you remember where to place your fingers and makes your chord changes much quicker. Full details in colour can be printed from the website **www.mikejackson.com.au**

Setting Up Your Ukulele

1. Buy a set of sticky coloured paper dots from a newsagency, or office/stationery supplier, and stick them onto the fretboard, <u>underneath</u> the strings, as shown here and on the back cover.

    You'll need red (R), yellow (Y) and green (G) dots.

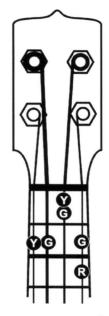

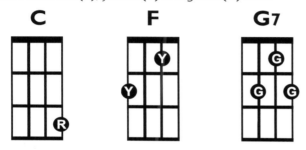

2. Stick another dot (of any colour) on the back of the ukulele neck — behind the second fret.

3. Tune your ukulele — see previous page

Setting Up The Song Book

4. Circle the chord names on the song pages with appropriately coloured highlighter pens:
    C = Red, F = Yellow, G7 = Green

    Ⓒ   G7   Ⓒ
    Go tell Aunt Rhody, go tell Aunt Rhody

Making Chords

Using your non-dominant hand, gently place your thumb — facing up, on the dot at the back of the fretboard.

Now use the tips of your fingers to gently press the strings onto the correct dots for the chord you are going to play. Make sure you use the correct finger for each dot and that your finger only touches the string that you are pressing down.

Finger numbering:
1 — index finger
2 — middle finger
3 — ring finger

Chord Diagrams

C Chord

Place your ring finger (3)
on the red dot.

F Chord

Place your pointer and
middle finger (1 & 2)
on the yellow dots.

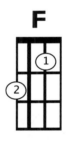

G7 Chord

Place your pointer finger (1)
on the green dot next to the first
yellow dot and place your middle
finger (2) and ring finger (3)
on the other green dots.

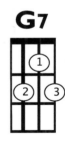

Hints

- Strings only have to touch the fret to change a note, so you don't need to press hard.
- Be patient! Give your hands plenty of time to learn new tricks and above all, relax when you're learning them. The more tense you are, the harder it becomes to learn and the more likely you are to make your fingers/hands sore.
- The skin on your finger tips will gradually become hardened — so play for short periods when you first begin.

Ukulele Chords Used in this Book

 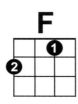

Ukulele as a Classroom Music Program

Ukuleles are wonderful instruments to use for a classroom music program.

- They are a very easy instrument to learn to play
- Children sing while they are playing
- Playing and learning an instrument as a class (as opposed to individual tuition) is a fun, social activity
- Instruments can be (hygienically) shared so a class set can be used by a whole school

- They sound good when played at this starter level
- The ukulele has comfortable physical attributes which allow it to be mastered by any age/size of child from age 4 onwards
- Entry level ukuleles come in bright colours which make them very attractive to children

Useful Tips for Teachers

Do not buy cheap ukuleles! They will not play or stay in tune. Spending a little more for a good quality entry-level ukulele will save money, time and pain on the ears later!

Buy a half-class set of ukes (1 instrument between 2 students) for a start and have the children working in pairs — one playing, the other one making sure the player has 'understood your instructions'. This ensures:

a. Students learn quicker by 'teaching'.
b. Less playing time avoids sore fingers
c. Students become eager to have their own instrument

Experience has shown that, once you start the playing bug, it spreads like wildfire through the school. You will need to specify the best brand/s of ukes for parents to buy and where to get them.

The 'Uke'n Play Book/CD's are both a method of learning the songs and a musical backing to play along with. Have copies in the school library for students to borrow and practise with.

Teach other staff members to play as well — then the ukes won't end up abandoned in a cupboard if/when you move on.

Obtain or create a ukulele arrangement of the National Anthem and your School Song — for assemblies and special occasions.

Encourage ensembles to form and present items in class and at assemblies.

Strumming

The ukulele, like the drum, must keep the beat so keep your strumming constant through the whole song. Begin by using 'down' strums or a 'down-up-down-up' strum and play with the back of your fingernail/s, side of your thumb, or a felt pick which can be purchased from a music shop.

Strum patterns (Track 27)

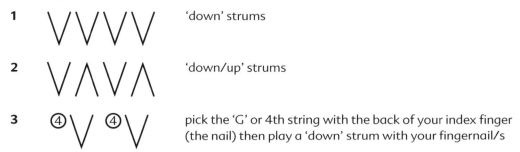

1   'down' strums

2   'down/up' strums

3   pick the 'G' or 4th string with the back of your index finger (the nail) then play a 'down' strum with your fingernail/s

Chord Patterns (Track 28)

Before playing any songs, try repeating these chord patterns with 4 strums on each chord. If a particular chord change is giving you trouble, slow down your strumming (or play 8 strums on each chord) and practise only that change until you are comfortable with it.

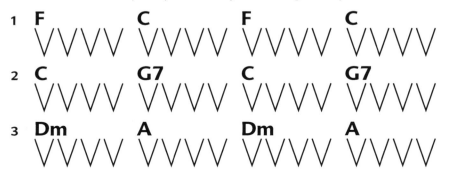

1   F   C   F   C

2   C   G7   C   G7

3   Dm   A   Dm   A

You can practise chord changes silently while watching TV! Just do the chord changes without strumming.

Other Options for Left Handed Players:

- Play a standard tuned ukulele 'right handed' (strum with your right hand) — chord shapes need no modification. **OR**
- Play a standard tuned ukulele 'left-handed' (strum with your left hand) — play the chords upside down.

Both these options will take extra effort in learning to play, but the benefit is that you will be able to play other ukuleles — without modification

1. Three Blind Mice

Traditional. This arrangement by Mike Jackson.

C
Three blind mice, three blind mice

C
See how they run, see how they run

C
They all ran after the farmer's wife

C
Who cut off their tails with a carving knife

C
Did ever you see such a thing in your life

C
As three blind mice?

REPEAT

Ring finger (3) on red dot

2. Life is But A Melancholy Flower

Traditional. This arrangement by Mike Jackson.

F
Life is but a ... Life is but a ...

F
Melancholy flower. Melancholy flower

F
Life is but a melon. Life is but a melon

F
Cauliflower. Cauliflower

Pointer (1) and middle (2) fingers on yellow dots

3. Miss Mary Mac

Traditional. This arrangement by Mike Jackson.

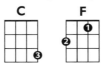

F
Miss Mary Mac, Mac, Mac

All dressed in black, black, black

With silver buttons, buttons, buttons

C
All down her back, back, back

She asked her mother, mother, mother

For 50 cents, cents, cents

To see the elephants, elephants, elephants

F
Jump over the fence, fence, fence

F
They jumped so high, high, high

They reached the sky, sky, sky

And they didn't came back, back, back

C
Till the 4th of July, ly, ly

Miss Mary Mac, Mac, Mac

All dressed in black, black, black

With silver buttons, buttons, buttons

F
All down her back, back, back

Pointer (1) and middle (2) fingers on yellow dots for F, then change to ring finger (3) on red dot for C

4. Polly Wolly Doodle

Traditional. Verse 3 & 4 Mike Jackson. This arrangement by Mike Jackson.

F
Oh, I went down south for to see my gal

C
Singing Polly Wolly Doodle all the day

My Sal she is a saucy gal

F
Singing Polly Wolly Doodle all the day

Strum no. 3 on page 9 can be used for this song

CHORUS:
F   **C**
Fare thee well, fare thee well, fare thee well, my fairy fay

For I'm goin' to Lousiana, for to see my Susyanna

F
Sing Polly Wolly Doodle all the day

C
Fare thee well, fare thee well, fare thee well, my fairy fay

For I'm goin' to Lousiana, for to see my Susyanna

F
Sing Polly Wolly Doodle all the day

F
Grasshopper sitting on a railroad track

C
Sing Polly Wolly Doodle all the day

He was picking his teeth with a carpet tack

F
Sing Polly Wolly Doodle all the day

CHORUS:

F
Our family went to the zoo to play

                                C
Sing Polly Wolly Doodle all the day

They asked my brother if he'd like to stay

                                F
Sing Polly Wolly Doodle all the day

    CHORUS

F
He's sometimes a monkey, that bit's true

                                C
Sing Polly Wolly Doodle all the day

But he helps feed the animals in the zoo

                                F
Sing Polly Wolly Doodle all the day

    CHORUS

5. He's Got The Whole World In His Hands

Traditional. This arrangement by Mike Jackson.

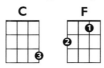

CHORUS:

F
He's got the whole world in His hands
          C
He's got the whole wide world in His hands
          F
He's got the whole world in His hands
         C   **F**
He's got the whole world in His hands

4 strums only on the C chord in the last line

F
He's got you and me brothers, in His hands
      C
He's got you and me brothers, in His hands
      F
He's got you and me brothers, in His hands
      C   **F**
He's got the whole world in His hands

CHORUS

F
He's got you and me sisters, in His hands
      C
He's got you and me sisters, in His hands
      F
He's got you and me sisters, in His hands
      C   **F**
He's got the whole world in His hands

CHORUS

6. Oh Dear What Can The Matter Be?

Traditional. This arrangement by Mike Jackson.

CHORUS:

F
Oh, dear! What can the matter be?
C
Dear, dear! What can the matter be?
F
Oh, dear! What can the matter be?
C   **F**
Johnny's so long at the fair

Strum in 3's for this song ie VVV VVV

F
He promised to buy me a trinket to please me
      C
And then for a smile, oh, he vowed he would tease me
      F
He promised to buy me a bunch of blue ribbons
      C   **F**
To tie up my bonnie brown hair

CHORUS

F
He promised to bring me a basket of posies
      C
A garland of lilies, a gift of red roses
      F
A little straw hat to set off the blue ribbons
      C   **F**
That tie up my bonnie brown hair

CHORUS

7. The Farmer's in The Dell

Traditional. This arrangement by Mike Jackson.

F
The farmer's in the dell, the farmer's in the dell
           C   **F**
Eee-i-addy-o, the farmer's in the dell

The farmer takes a wife, the farmer takes a wife
           C   **F**
Eee-i-addy-o, the farmer takes a wife

The wife takes a child, the wife takes a child
           C   **F**
Eee-i-addy-o, the wife takes a child

F
The child takes the dog, the child takes the dog
           C   **F**
Eee-i-addy-o, the child takes the dog

The dog takes the cat, the dog takes the cat
           C   **F**
Eee-i-addy-o, the dog takes the cat

The cat takes the mouse, the cat takes the mouse
           C   **F**
Eee-i-addy-o, the cat takes the mouse

F
The mouse takes the cheese, the mouse takes the cheese
           C   **F**
Eee-i-addy-o, the mouse takes the cheese

F
The cheese stands alone!!

2 strums only on every C chord

8. It Ain't Gonna Rain No More

Traditional. This arrangement by Mike Jackson.

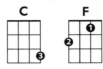

CHORUS:

F
It ain't gonna' rain no more, no more

C
It ain't gonna' rain no more

How in the heck can I wash my neck

F
When the wash rag's on the floor

F
We had a cat down on our farm

C
It ate a ball of yarn

When those little kittens were born

F
They all had sweaters on

CHORUS

F
We had a goat down on our farm

C
It ate up old tin cans

And when those little goats were born

F
They came in Ford sedans

CHORUS x 2

9. London Bridge is Falling Down

Traditional. This arrangement by Mike Jackson.

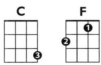

F
London Bridge is falling down
C   **F**
Falling down, falling down

London Bridge is falling down
C   **F**
My fair lady

F
Build it up with sticks and stones
C   **F**
Sticks and stones, sticks and stones

Build it up with sticks and stones
C   **F**
My fair lady

F
Sticks and stones will wash away
C   **F**
Wash away, wash away

Sticks and stones will wash away
C   **F**
My fair lady

Try strum no. 3 on page 9 for this song

F
Build it up with iron and steel
C   **F**
Iron and steel, iron and steel

Build it up with iron and steel
C   **F**
My fair lady

F
Iron and steel will bend and bow
C   **F**
Bend and bow, bend and bow

Iron and steel will bend and bow
C   **F**
My fair lady

REPEAT VERSE 1

10. Li'l Liza Jane

Traditional. This arrangement by Mike Jackson.

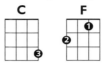

F
I've got a gal and you've got none, Li'l Liza Jane

                         C   **F**
I've got a gal that calls me "Hon'," Li'l Liza Jane

CHORUS:
F
Oh, Eliza, Li'l Liza Jane

       C   **F**
Oh, Eliza, Li'l Liza Jane

F
Come, my love, and live with me, Li'l Liza Jane

                  C   **F**
I will take good care of thee, Li'l Liza Jane

CHORUS

F
Liza Jane has come to me, Li'l Liza Jane

             C   **F**
We're as happy as can be, Li'l Liza Jane

CHORUS

F
We have a house in Baltimore, Li'l Liza Jane

                 C   **F**
Lots of children 'round the door, Li'l Liza Jane

CHORUS X 2

Strum no. 3 on page 9 is good for this song too

11. Down In The Valley

Traditional. This arrangement by Mike Jackson.

F   **C**
Down in the valley, the valley so low

                               F
Hang your head over, hear the wind blow

                                    C
Hear the wind blow, dear, hear the wind blow

                               F
Hang your head over, hear the wind blow

F   **C**
Writing this letter, containing this line

                           F
Answer my question, will you be mine?

                           C
Will you be mine, dear, will you be mine?

                             F
Please answer my question, will you be mine?

F   **C**
Write me a letter, send it by mail

                           F
Send it in care of the Birmingham jail

                           C
Birmingham jail, dear, Birmingham jail

                           F
Send it in care of the Birmingham jail

REPEAT VERSE I

Strum in 3's for this song again ie VVV VVV

12. Blow The Man Down

Traditional. This arrangement by Mike Jackson.

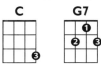

C
Come all you young fellows that follows the sea

G7
To me way, hey, blow the man down!

Now please pay attention and listen to me

C
Give me some time to blow the man down

Ring finger (3) on red dot for C then change to fingers 1, 2 and 3 on green dots for G7

CHORUS:

C
Blow the man down bullies, blow the man down

G7
To me way, hey, blow the man down!

Blow her right back home to Liverpool Town

C
Oh, give me some time to blow the man down

C
On a trim Black Ball liner, I first served me time

G7
To me way, hey, blow the man down!

On a trim Black ball liner, I wasted me prime

C
Oh, give me some time to blow the man down

CHORUS

C
When a trim Black Ball liner's preparing for sea

        G7
To me way, hey, blow the man down!

You'd split your sides laughing, such sights you would see

        C
Oh, give me some time to blow the man down

CHORUS
C
Well, there are tinkers and tailors and cobblers and all

        G7
To me way, hey, blow the man down!

They're all shipped for sailors on board the Black Ball

        C
Oh, give me some time to blow the man down

CHORUS

A ¾ song again —
strum in 3's

13. Go Tell Aunt Rhody

Traditional. This arrangement by Mike Jackson.

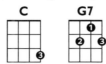

CHORUS:

C   G7   C
Go tell Aunt Rhody, go tell Aunt Rhody
          G7   C
Go tell Aunt Rhody the old grey goose is dead

C   G7   C
The one she's been saving, the one she's been saving
           G7   C
The one she's been saving to make a feather bed

CHORUS

C   G7   C
She died in the millpond, she died in the millpond
         G7   C
She died in the millpond standing on her head

CHORUS x 2

14. Michael Finnigan

Traditional. This arrangement by Mike Jackson.

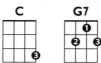

C
There was an old man called Michael Finnigan
G7
He grew whiskers on his chin again
    C
The wind came out and blew them in again
G7   **C**
Poor old Michael Finnigan, begin again

Try strum no. 3 on page 9 for this song

C
There was an old man called Michael Finnigan
    G7
Who went off fishing with a pin again
C
Caught a fish, but it fell in again
G7   **C**
Poor old Michael Finnigan, begin again

C
There was an old man called Michael Finnigan
G7
He grew fat and he grew thin again
C
Then he died, and had to begin again
G7   **C**
Poor old Michael Finnigan

REPEAT WHOLE SONG

15. Clementine

Traditional. This arrangement by Mike Jackson.

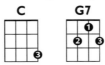

C
In a cavern, in a canyon

      G7
Excavating for a mine

          C
Dwelt a miner – Forty-niner

G7   **C**
And his daughter Clementine

CHORUS:
C
Oh my darling, oh my darling

         G7
Oh my darling, Clementine

         C
Thou art lost and gone forever

G7   **C**
Dreadful sorry, Clementine

C
Light she was and like a fairy

        G7
And her shoes were number nine

      C
Herring boxes without topses

G7   **C**
Sandals were for Clementine

CHORUS

C
Drove she ducklings to the water
                        G7
Every morning just at nine
                        C
Tripped her foot against a splinter
   G7   **C**
Fell into the foaming brine

CHORUS

C
Saw her lips above the water
                       G7
Blowing bubbles mighty fine
                 C
But alas, I was no swimmer
   G7   **C**
So I lost my Clementine

CHORUS

16. Down By The Billabong (Station)

Verse 1 trad; additional verses Mike Jackson and Michelle Freeman. Traditional. This arrangement by Mike Jackson

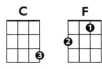

2 strums only on every F chord

C   **F**   **C**
Down by the billabong, early in the morning
                          F   **C**
See the cockatoos sitting all in a row
                             F   **C**
See them preen their feathers then stick their yellow combs up
                  F   **C**
Screech screech, flap flap, off they go

C   **F**   **C**
Down by the billabong, early in the morning
                    F   **C**
See the little wallabies all in a row
                        F   **C**
See them sniff the air then turn their little ears round
                 F   **C**
Hop hop, bounce bounce, off they go

C   **F**   **C**
Down by the station, early in the morning
                 F   **C**
See the little engines all in a row
                     F   **C**
See the engine driver turn the little handle
             F   **C**
Puff, puff, toot toot, off we go

17. Skip To My Lou, My Darling

Traditional. This arrangement by Mike Jackson.

C
Fly's in the buttermilk, shoo, fly, shoo
G7
Fly's in the buttermilk, shoo, fly, shoo
C
Fly's in the buttermilk, shoo, fly, shoo
G7   **C**
Skip to my Lou, my darlin'

CHORUS:

    C
    Lou, Lou, skip to my Lou
    G7
    Lou, Lou, skip to my Lou
    C
    Lou, Lou, skip to my Lou
    G7   **C**
    Skip to my Lou, my darlin'

C
Cat's in the cream jar, ooh, ooh, ooh
G7
Cat's in the cream jar, ooh, ooh, ooh
C
Cat's in the cream jar, ooh, ooh, ooh
G7   **C**
Skip to my Lou, my darlin'

CHORUS x 2

18. Hail! Hail! The Gang's All Here

P.D. This arrangement by Mike Jackson

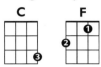

CHORUS:

F
Hail! Hail! The gang's all here
C
What the heck do we care?

What the heck do we care?
F
Hail! Hail! We're full of cheer
C   **F**
What the heck do we care Bill!

F
A gang of good fellows are we (are we)

Are we (are we) are we (are we)

With never a worry you see (you see)
    C
You see (you see) you see (you see)
                F   **C**   **F**
We'll sing till morn and never yawn, we'll live life merrily
    C
No matter the weather, when we get together
   F   **C**
We have a jubilee

CHORUS

      F
When out for a good time we go, (we go)

We go, (we go) we go, (we go)

There's nothing we do that is slow, (is slow)
    C
Is slow, (is slow) is slow, (is slow)
                 F   **C**   **F**
Of joy we get our share you bet, the gang will tell you so
    C
No matter the weather, when we get together
    F   **C**
We sing this song you know

CHORUS

19. Sur Le Pont D'Avignon

Traditional. This arrangement by Mike Jackson

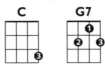

C   **G7**
Sur le pont d'Avignon

C   **G7**
L'on y danse, l'on y danse

C   **G7**
Sur le pont d'Avignon

C   **G7**   **C**
L'on y danse tous en rond

          G7   **C**
Les beaux messieurs font comm' çà

         G7   **C**
Et puis encore comm' çà

Practise 4 strums on C the 4 strums on G7 and repeat for the first 3 lines of each verse

C   **G7**
Sur le pont d'Avignon

C   **G7**
L'on y danse, l'on y danse

C   **G7**
Sur le pont d'Avignon

C   **G7**   **C**
L'on y danse tous en rond

          G7   **C**
Les bell' dames font comm' çà

         G7   **C**
Et puis encore comm' çà

C   **G7**
Sur le pont d'Avignon

C   **G7**
L'on y danse, l'on y danse

C   **G7**
Sur le pont d'Avignon

C   **G7**   **C**
L'on y danse tous en rond

                      G7   **C**
Les jardiniers font comm' çà

                G7   **C**
Et puis encore comm' çà

C   **G7**
Sur le pont d'Avignon

C   **G7**
L'on y danse, l'on y danse

C   **G7**
Sur le pont d'Avignon

C   **G7**   **C**
L'on y danse tous en rond

REPEAT LAST SECTION X 2

20. The Ballad Of Eensy Weensy

Words: Chorus Traditional; Verses Mike Jackson. Music: Traditional. This arrangement by Mike Jackson

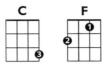

CHORUS:

C   F   C
Eensy Weensy Spider climbed up the waterspout

                            F   C
Down came the rain and washed poor Eensy out

F   C   F
Out came the sunshine and dried up all the rain

           C   F   C
So the Eensy Weensy Spider climbed up the spout again

C   F   C
The spider climbed the spout and she gave a little cheer

                     F   C
I'm almost at the top and my journey's end is near

F   C   F
Then she heard a clap of thunder and down came lots of rain

          C   F   C
And both she and all her hopes went sadly down the drain

C   F   C
As she lay there at the bottom the poor spider felt quite done

                              F   C
But, as very often happens, after rain there came the sun

F   C F
The Eensy Weensy Spider soon was warm and dry

     C   F   C
So she headed for the spout again to have another try

CHORUS

```
C                          F              C
The moral of this story is one I'm sure you know

                                    F         C
If you don't make it the first time then have another go

      F          C              F
And take a little lesson from the spider in this song

        C                    F            C
Then if you're at the bottom, you won't stay there for long
```

21. Rock My Soul

Traditional. This arrangement by Mike Jackson

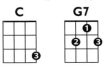

CHORUS 1:

C
I'm gonna rock my soul in the bosom of Abraham
G7   **C**
Rock my soul in the bosom of Abraham

Rock my soul in the bosom of Abraham
G7   **C**
Oh, rock my soul

CHORUS 2:

C
I'm gonna rock, rock, rock, my soul
         G7   **C**
I'm gonna rock, rock, rock, my soul

I'm gonna rock, rock, rock, my soul
       G7   **C**
In the bosom of Abraham

C
I may be weak (Rock my soul)

But though art strong (Rock my soul)

I'm leaning on (Rock my soul)
           G7   **C**
I'm leaning on His mighty arm

CHORUS 1 & 2

C
My soul is glad (Rock my soul)

My sins are free (Rock my soul)

I'm going home (Rock my soul)
                G7 C
I'm going home to liberty

CHORUS 1 X 2

22. Mary Had A Little Lamb

Traditional. This arrangement by Mike Jackson.

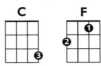

F   C   F
Mary had a little lamb, little lamb, little lamb

            C   F
Mary had a little lamb whose feet were black as soot

           C   F
Everywhere that Mary went, Mary went, Mary went

           C   F
Everywhere that Mary went it put its sooty foot

F   C   F
Mary had another lamb, 'nother lamb, 'nother lamb

            C   F
Mary had another lamb whose fleas were white as snow

             C   F
And everywhere that Mary went, Mary went, Mary went

           C   F
Everywhere that Mary went the fleas were sure to go

F   C   F
Mary had a little lamb, little lamb, little lamb

           C   F
Mary had a little lamb its fleece was white as snow

23. Aloutte

Traditional. This arrangement by Mike Jackson.

F   **C**   **F**   **C**   **F**
Alouette, gentile Alouette. Alouette je te plumerai
F   **C**   **F**   **C**   **F**
Alouette, gentille Alouette. Alouette je te plumerai
F   **C**   **F**
Je te plumerai la tête. Je te plumerai la tête
C
Et la tête, et la tête. Alouette, Alouette
C
O-o-o-o-oh

F   **C**   **F**   **C**   **F**
Alouette, gentille Alouette. Alouette je te plumerai
F   **C**   **F**   **C**   **F**
Alouette, gentille Alouette. Alouette je te plumerai
F   **C**   **F**
Je te plumerai le nez. Je te plumerai le nez
C
Et le nez, et le nez. Alouette, Alouette
C
O-o-o-o-oh

F   **C**   **F**   **C**   **F**
Alouette, gentille Alouette. Alouette je te plumerai
F   **C**   **F**   **C**   **F**
Alouette, gentille Alouette. Alouette je te plumerai
F   **C**   **F**
Je te plumerai les yeux. Je te plumerai les yeux
C
Et les yeux, et les yeux. Alouette, Alouette
C
O-o-o-o-oh
F   **C**   **F**   **C**   **F**
Alouette, gentille Alouette. Alouette je te plumerai

24. I's The B'y That Builds The Boat

Traditional. This arrangement by Mike Jackson

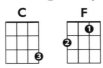

CHORUS:

F   **C**
I's the b'y that builds the boat

F   **C**
I's the b'y that sails her

F   **C**
I's the b'y that catches the fish

                    F
And takes them home to Liza

F   **C**
Hip yer partner, Sally Thibault

F   **C**
Swing yer partner, Sally Brown

F   **C**
Fogo, Twillingate, Morton's Harbour

               F
All around the circle!

F   **C**
Sods and rinds to cover your flake

F   **C**
Cake and tea for supper

F   **C**
Codfish in the Spring o' the year

               F
Fried in maggoty butter

CHORUS

F   C
I took Liza to a dance
F   C
And faith, but she could travel
F   C
And every step that she did take
                      F
She was up to her knees in gravel

     CHORUS

F   C
Susan White, she's out of sight
F   C
Her petticoat wants a border
F   C
Old Sam Oliver in the dark
                F
He kissed her in the corner

     CHORUS X 2

25. Joshua Fought The Battle Of Jericho

Traditional. This arrangement by Mike Jackson

Dm

A

CHORUS:

Dm
Joshua fought the Battle of Jericho

A   **Dm**
Jericho, Jericho

Joshua fought the Battle of Jericho

          A   **Dm**
And the walls came tumbling down

Dm
You may talk about your men of Gideon

                   A
You may brag about your men of Saul

         Dm
But there's none like good old Joshua

      A   **Dm**
At the Battle of Jericho (Hear me calling now)

CHORUS

Dm
Up to the walls of Jericho

                A
He marched with spear in hand

   Dm
Go blow those ram horns, Joshua cried

      A   **Dm**
'Cause the battle is in my hands

CHORUS

2 new chords!
Firstly, practise chord pattern no. 3 on page 9

Middle finger (2) stays on its dot all the time

Dm
Then the lamb ram horns began to blow

                A
The trumpets began to sound

Dm
Joshua commanded the people to shout

     A   **Dm**
And the walls came tumblin' down (Hear me calling now)

CHORUS x 2

Similarity between Ukulele and Guitar

Remove the two thickest strings from a 6 string guitar and you create a tenor guitar. Now you have only 4 strings to worry about, the chords are the same but they become easier to play.

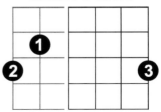
Guitar G Chord
Ukulele C Chord

Shorten your tenor guitar a little and you have a baritone ukulele — same 4 strings, same fingerwork.

Shorten your baritone ukulele and tune the strings up — you have a tenor, concert or soprano ukulele. The same fingering works but it now sounds higher, just as it would if you clipped a capo over the strings on the 5th fret of your guitar.

As standard ukulele C tuning is 5 notes higher than standard guitar tuning:

- Guitar G chord will be a C chord on the ukulele
- Guitar C chord will be an F chord on the ukulele
- Guitar D7 chord will be a G7 chord on the ukulele

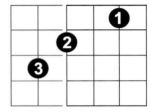
Guitar C Chord
Ukulele F Chord

The little soprano ukulele is by far the most common of the family. Its slightly larger cousins, the concert ukulele and the biggest of the three, the tenor ukulele, are most often tuned to the same notes. Their increased size alters the tone and the longer fretboard gives access to more notes - but they cost more and don't fit so easily in a backpack! Before buying, check the sound of bigger ukes and consider want you want to use it for — bigger is not always better.

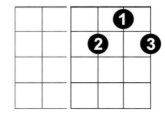
Guitar D7 Chord
Ukulele G7 Chord

Reading Guitar Chord Boxes for the Ukulele

You've just found your favourite song in a book featuring pictures of guitar chords (chord boxes).

If you're going to play solo you could treat the pictures as ukulele chord boxes by ignoring the two left hand strings as shown above.

If you're playing a baritone ukulele, you will now be playing the chords as written.

If you are playing a soprano, concert or tenor ukulele and others are playing with you, you will need to play the chords on the sheet music by their letter name instead of following the pictures. If you haven't already learned their shapes it's a good idea to have a ukulele chord chart with you.

The Play-along CD

The Play-along CD has recordings of all the songs in the book. It provides an easy way to learn the songs while giving you a lead vocal and ukulele to follow and a band of musicians to back you. The tempo of the songs is lively and they are played at their normal speed to keep the CD tracks enjoyable to listen to.

To Use the CD
Without the ukulele:
1 Listen to the CD as often as you can to learn the lyrics and tunes
2 Using the book and CD, sing the chord colour names to the tune of the song you are learning

    eg. London Bridge would go like this:

F
yellow, yellow, yellow, yellow
C   **F**
red red red, yellow yellow

yellow, yellow, yellow, yellow
C   **F**
red red, yellow

With the ukulele:
3 Without strumming, sing the chord names with the CD while 'playing' the chord shapes and getting used to changing between chords.

4 Now try strumming the song while singing as you did in Stage 3. If you find the CD tempo too fast, switch the CD off for a while, slow everything down and repeat until you are more comfortable.

5 Slowly bring the song up to speed as your skill improves.

6 Play along with the CD at speed and, when you can, sing the real words.

Also available...

Visit your local music shop or, in case of difficulty,
contact the Marketing Department, Music Sales Limited,
Newmarket Road, Bury St Edmunds, Suffolk, IP33 3YB, UK
marketing@musicsales.co.uk

About the Authors

Mike and Diane Jackson, have spent a large part of their life inspiring, encouraging and empowering music making in people of all ages.

A self-taught musician who plays 16 different instruments — including ukulele, Mike Jackson is perhaps best known for his hit version of Bananas in Pyjamas.

He has sold over 250,000 albums, published many song and dance resources and has performed extensively across Australia and Internationally. Mike's inspirational concerts and workshops attest to his belief that learning to play music is an attainable goal for everyone and that it's never, ever too late — or too early — to begin!

Diane has a Graduate Diploma in Music Education and many years experience teaching classroom music and taking community music classes for young children.

By using the 'Uke'n Play Ukulele' resource, many — who previously thought of themselves as being 'not musical' — have now fulfilled a lifelong dream of being able to play a musical instrument. Here's what some have said:

> Our ukuleles have had a good workout since the workshop. My wife and I now have uke hour each night after tea and play along with your CD. — Matt

> I joined one of the workshops with a little pink uke I bought for my daughter, plus the book and CD. I am not musical however I am now playing recognizable tunes. — Dean

> I have been having so much fun with it (uke and book/CD) and I am also a grandmother of four, so there is huge potential for many musical moments in my home. — Lyn

> The parents were amazed at what these children were achieving on the ukulele and many have made enquiries as to how and where to purchase an instrument. Hooray! We will have even more students with their own instruments playing and enjoying music. — Lorna

> On behalf of our little uke group in Footscray, we all wanted to say thank you for your book 'Uke'n Play Ukulele'. It was the book we ALL learnt from and it inspired us!

> I have picked up a copy of the book and CD and have loaned it to my mother, who is learning the uke to get her hands moving. She likes it and I hope I can get it back one day. — Bill

www.mikejackson.com.au

On The CD

1. Three Blind Mice

2. Life Is But A Melancholy Flower

3. Miss Mary Mac

4. Polly Wolly Doodle

5. He's Got The Whole World In His Hands

6. Oh, Dear! What Can The Matter Be?

7. The Farmer's In The Dell

8. It Ain't Gonna Rain No More

9. London Bridge Is Falling Down

10. Li'l Liza Jane

11. Down In The Valley

12. Blow The Man Down

13. Go Tell Aunt Rhody

14. Michael Finnigan

15. Clementine

16. Down By The Billabong (Station)

17. Skip To My Lou, My Darling

18. Hail! Hail! The Gang's All Here

19. Sur Le Pont D'Avignon

20. The Ballad Of Eensy Weensy

21. Rock My Soul

22. Mary Had A Little Lamb

23. Alouette

24. I's The B'y That Builds The Boat

25. Joshua Fought The Battle Of Jericho

26. Tuning Track

27. Strumming Track

28. Chord Pattern Track

All tracks
(Traditional/Jackson)
Larrikin Music Publishing